POP PIANO HITS

SIMPLE ARRANGEMENTS FOR STUDENTS OF ALL AGES

How Far I'll Go, This Town & More Hot Singles

ISBN 978-1-4950-8540-6

HAL•LEONARD®

7777 W. BLUEMOUND RD. P.O. BOX 13819 MILWAUKEE, WI 53213

Visit Hal Leonard Online at
www.halleonard.com

HOW FAR I'LL GO

from MOANA
as performed by Alessia Cara

Words and Music by
LIN-MANUEL MIRANDA

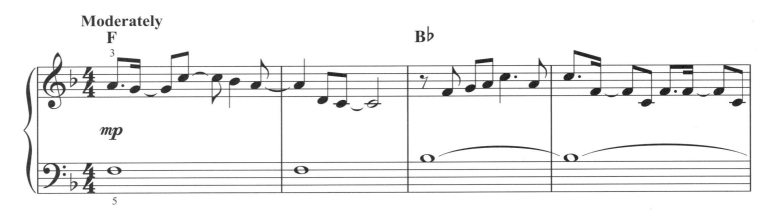

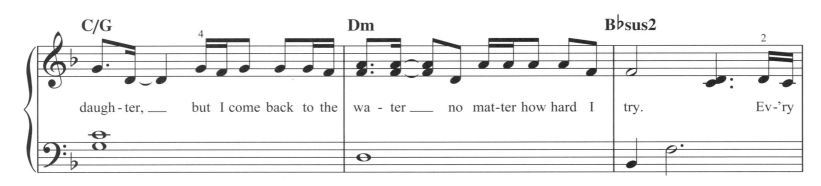

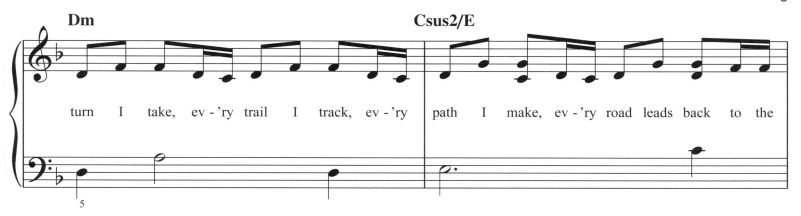

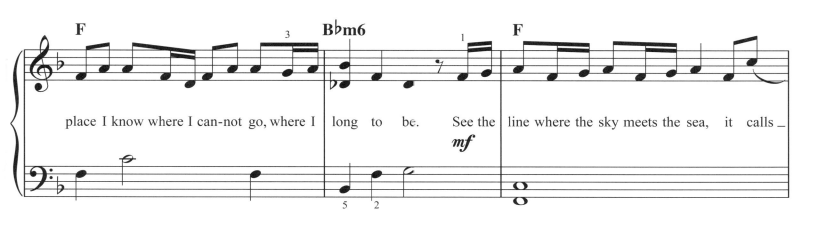

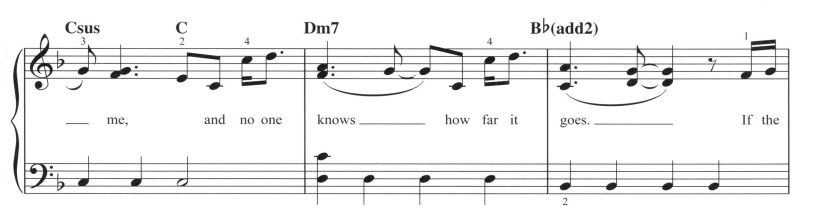

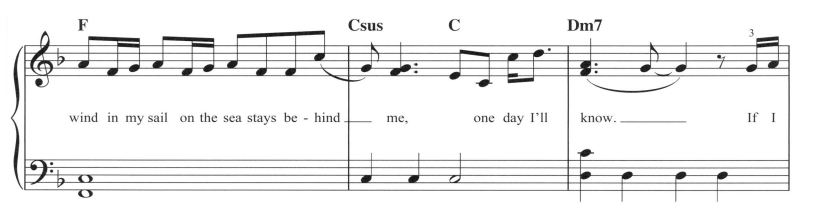

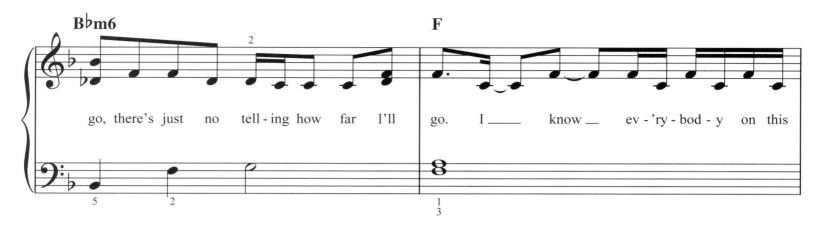

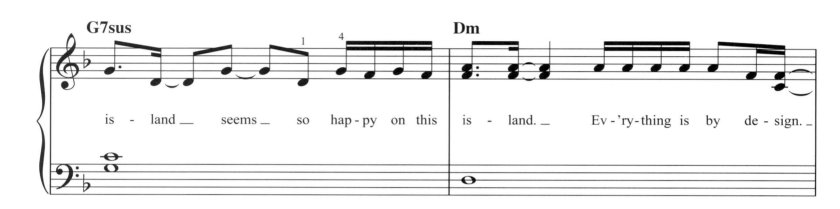

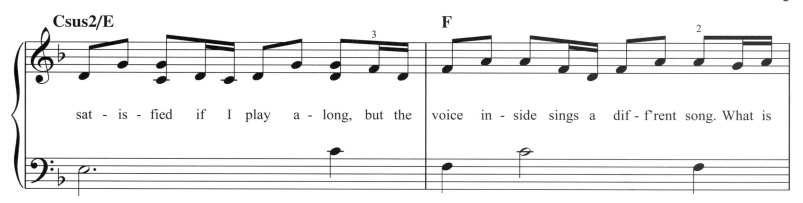

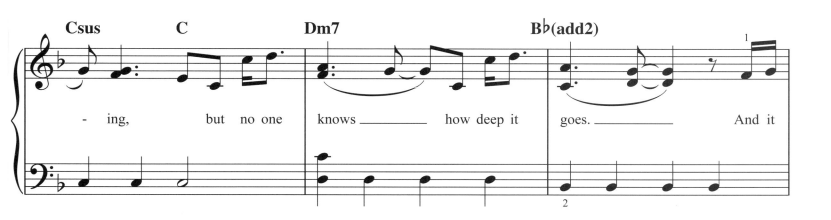

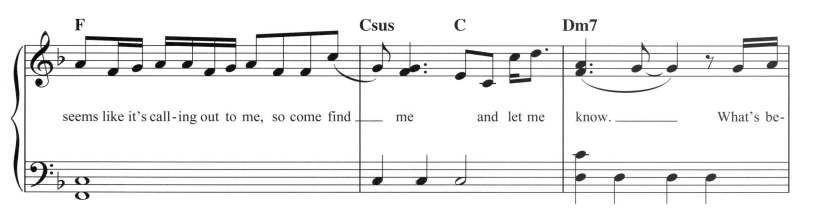

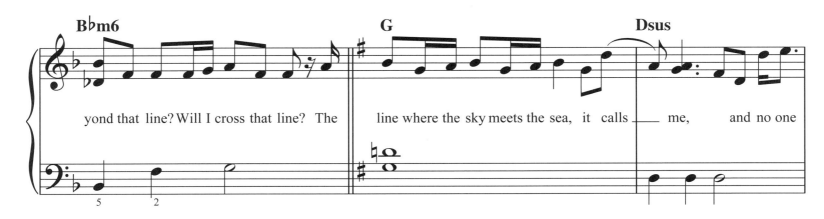

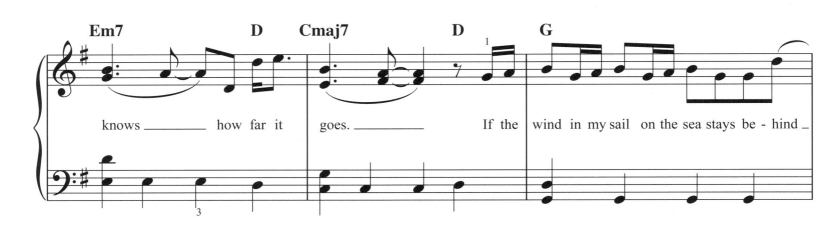

THIS TOWN

Words and Music by MIKE NEEDLE,
DANIEL BRYER, JAMIE SCOTT
and NIALL HORAN

Moderate Folk feel

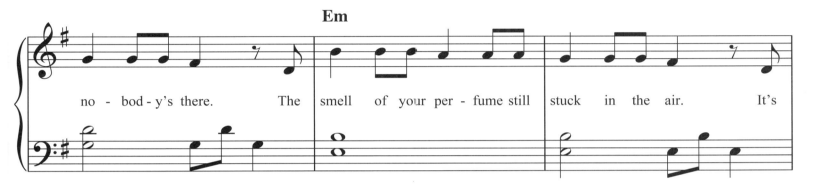

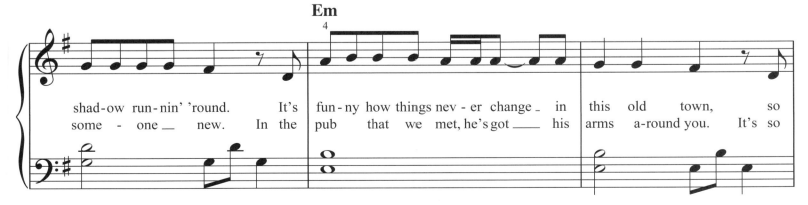

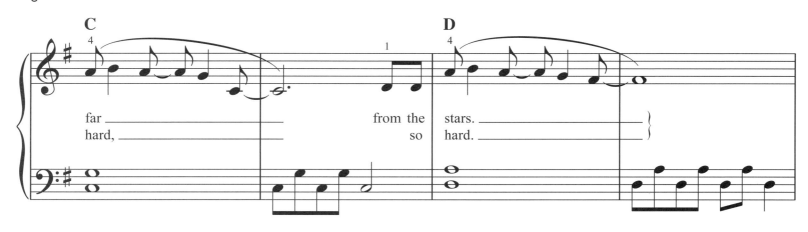

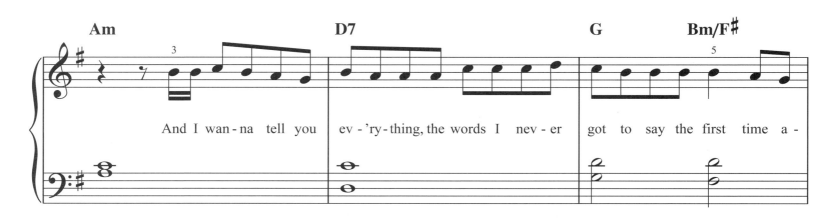

If the whole world was watch - ing, I'd still dance with you; drive

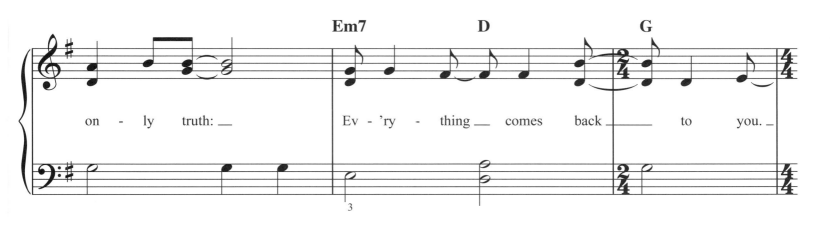

high - ways and by - ways to be there with you. O - ver and o - ver, the

on - ly truth: __ Ev - 'ry - thing __ comes back __ to you. __

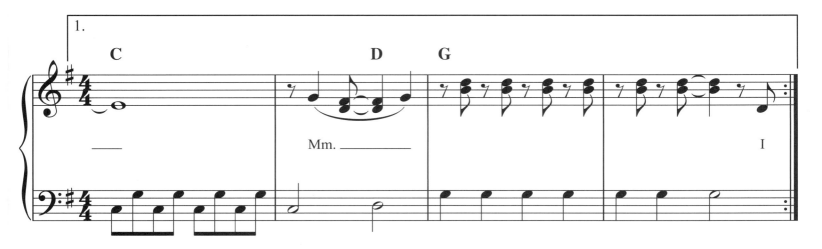

Mm. __ I

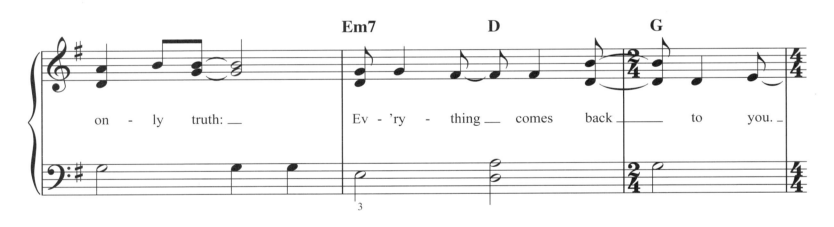

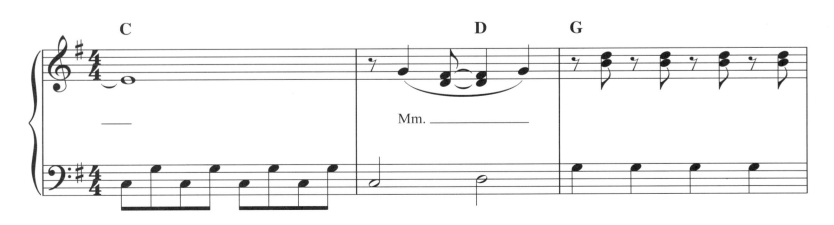

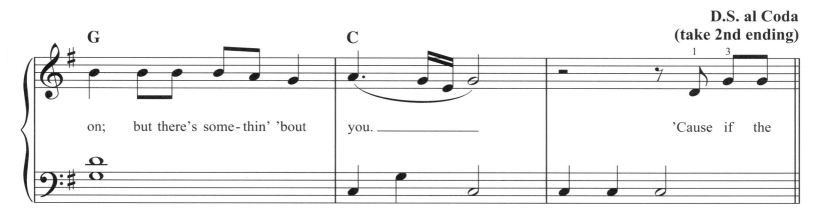

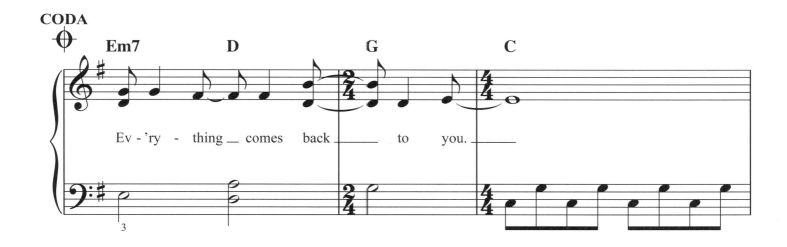

MY WAY

Words and Music by
CALVIN HARRIS

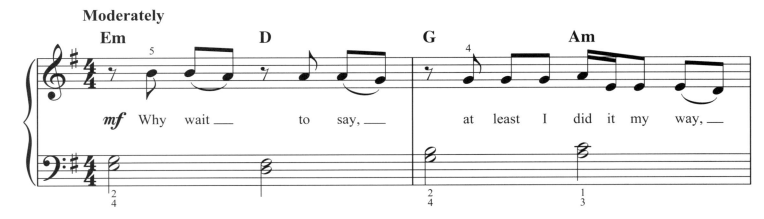

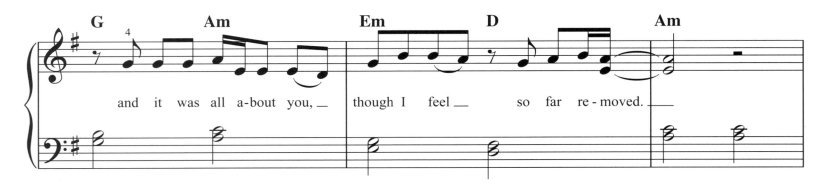

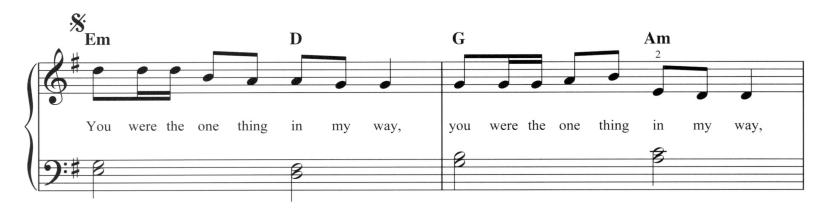

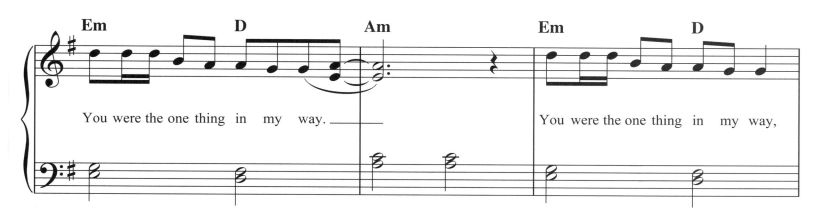

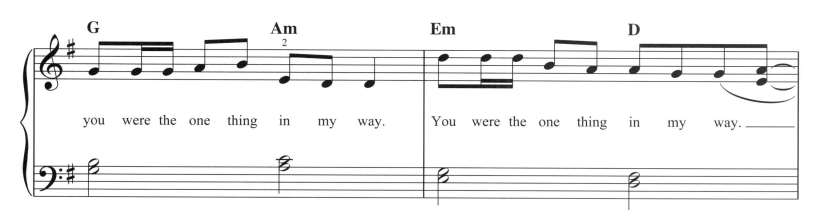

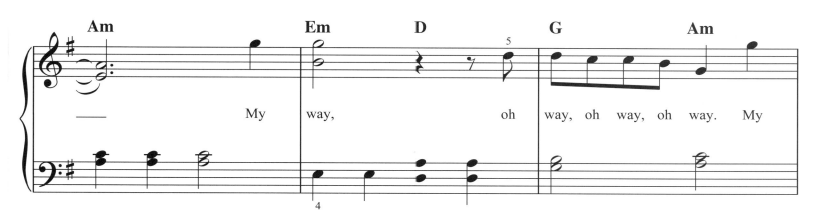

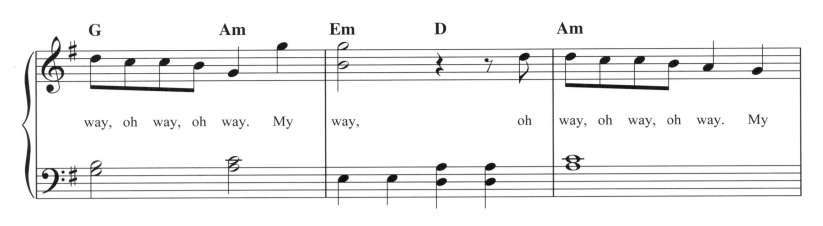

way, oh way, oh way. My way, oh way, oh way, oh way. My

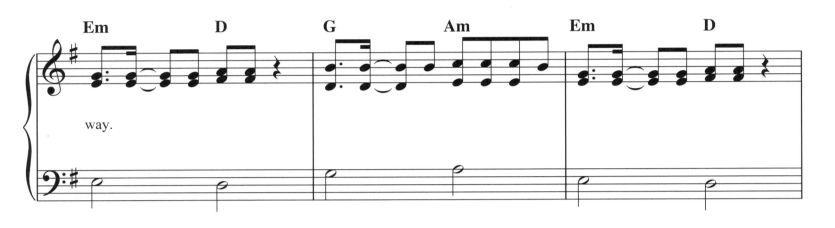

way.

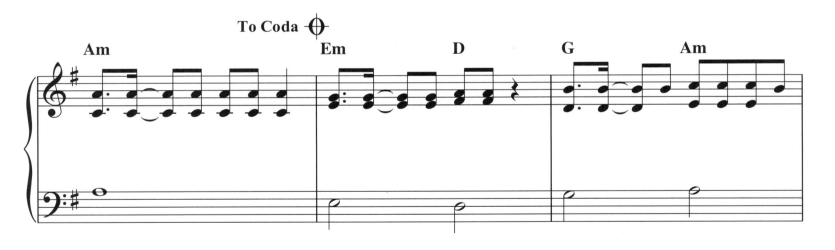

To Coda ⊕

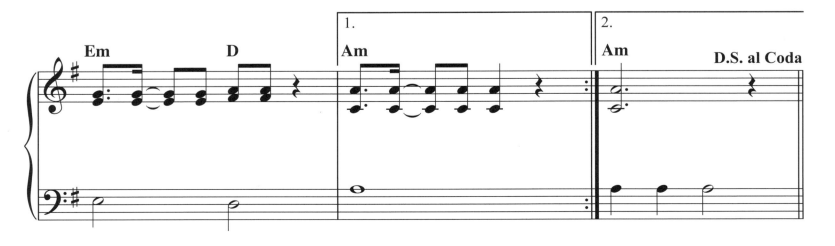

D.S. al Coda

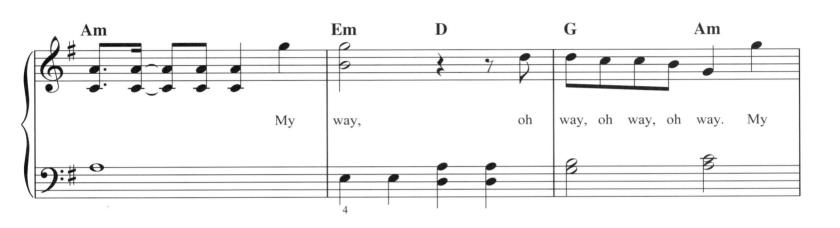

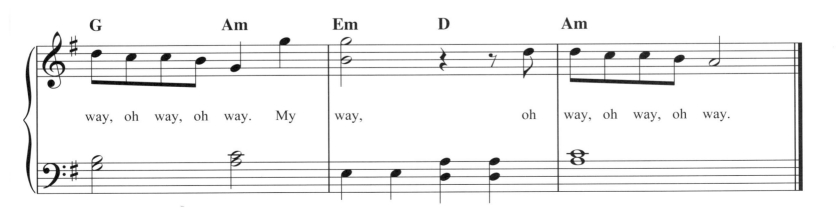

WE DON'T TALK ANYMORE

Words and Music by CHARLIE PUTH,
JACOB KASHIR HINDLIN and SELENA GOMEZ

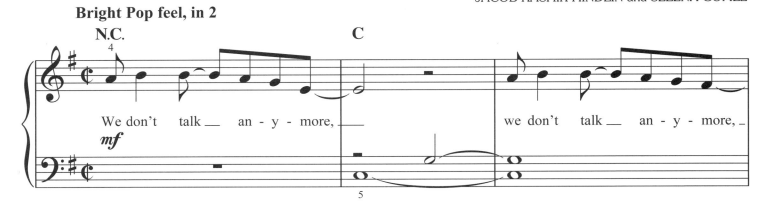

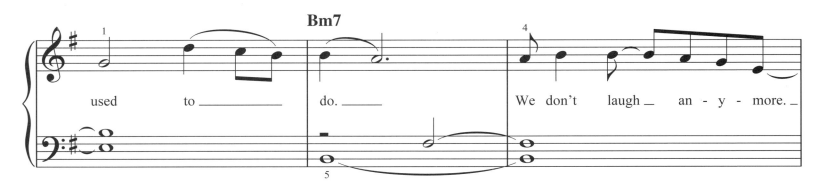

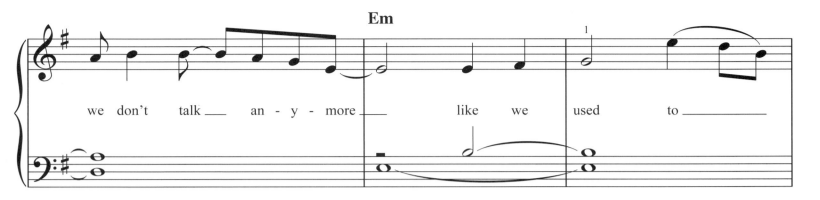

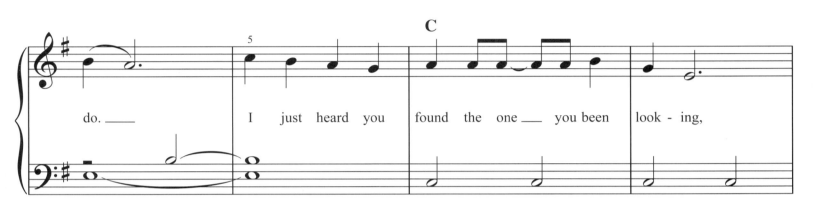

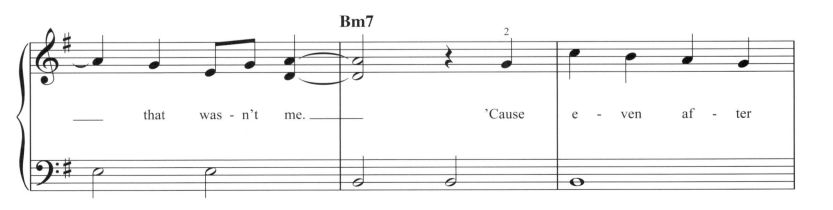

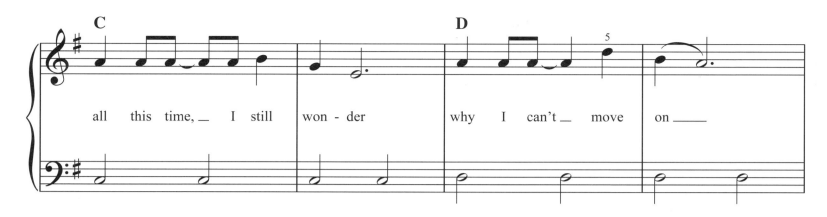

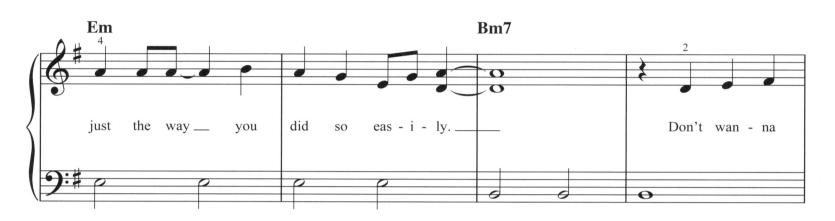

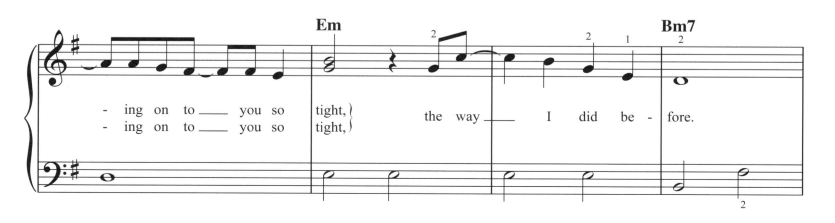

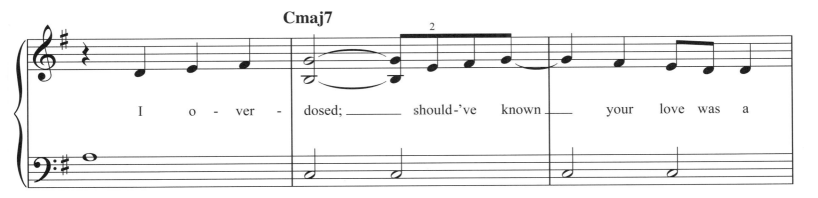

I o - ver - dosed; should-'ve known your love was a

game. Now I can't get you out of my brain. Ooh,

it's such a shame that we don't talk an - y - more,

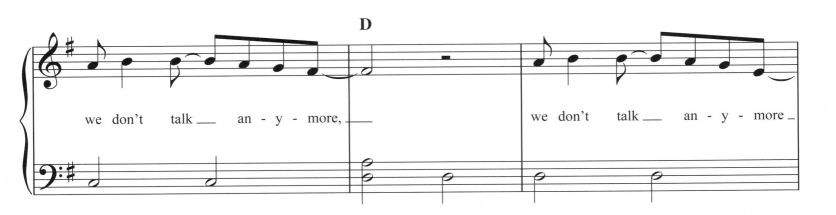

we don't talk an - y - more, we don't talk an - y - more

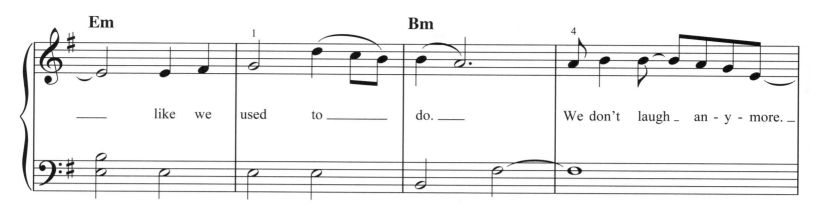

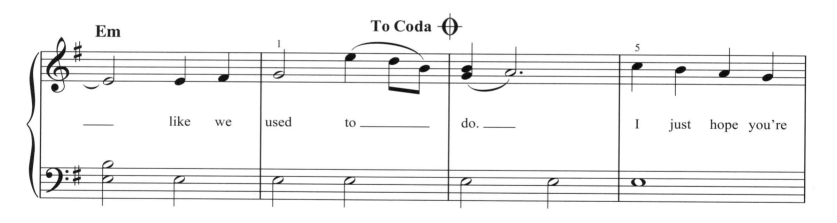

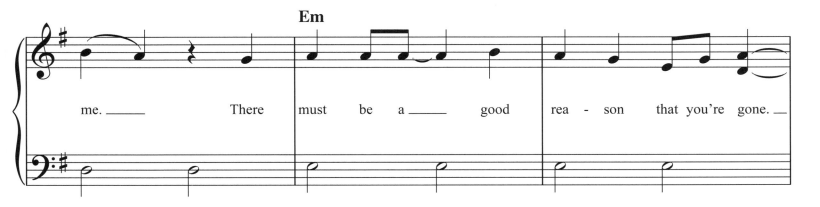

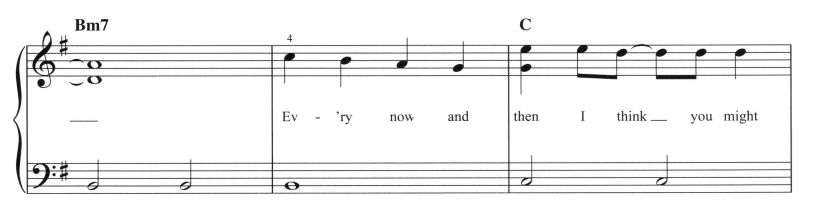

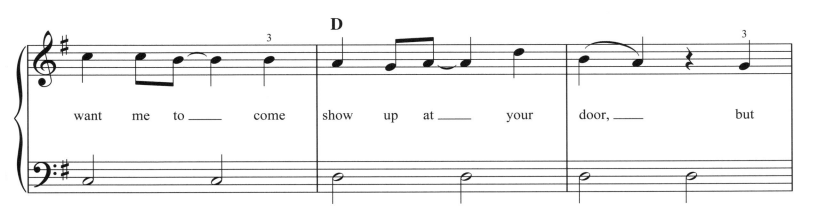

22

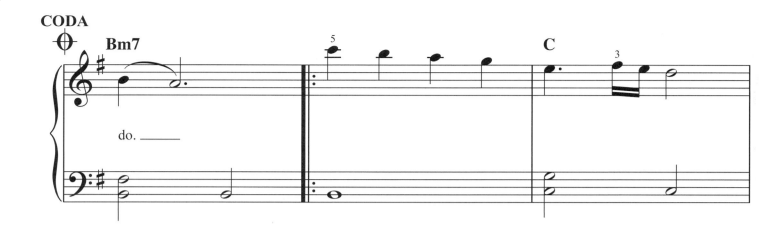

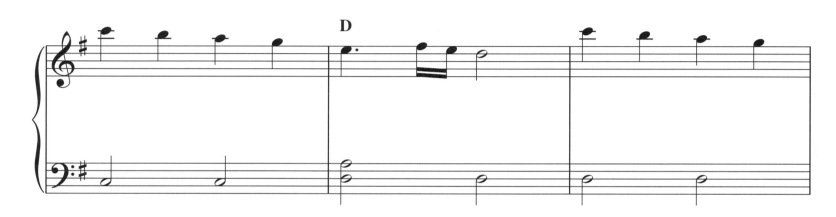

Don't wan - na know what kind of dress you're wear - ing to -

night, if he's giv - ing it to ___ you just right, the way ___

___ I did be - fore. I o - ver - dosed; ___ should-'ve known ___

___ your love was a game. Now I can't ___ get you out ___ of my

brain. Ooh, ___ it's such a shame ___ that

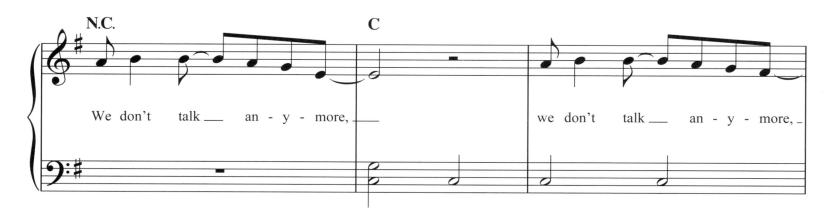

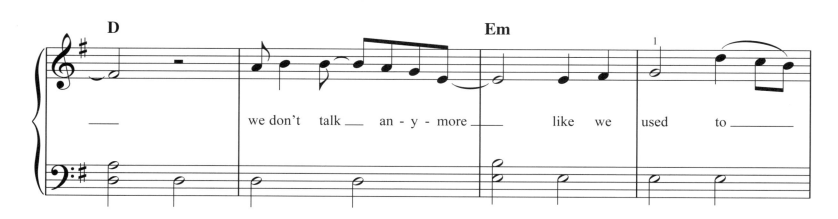

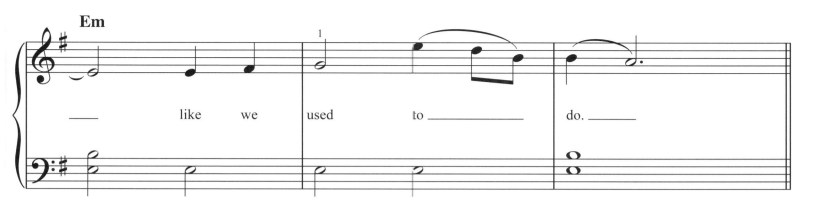

like we used to _____ do. _____

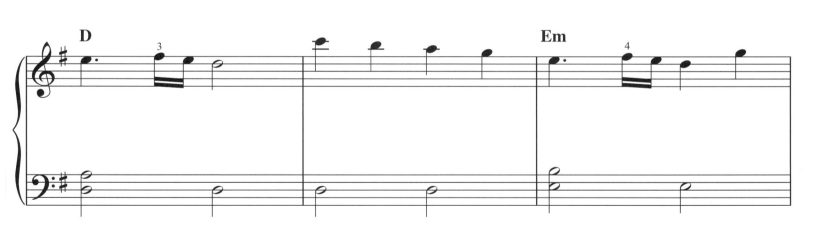

We don't talk ___ an - y - more. _____

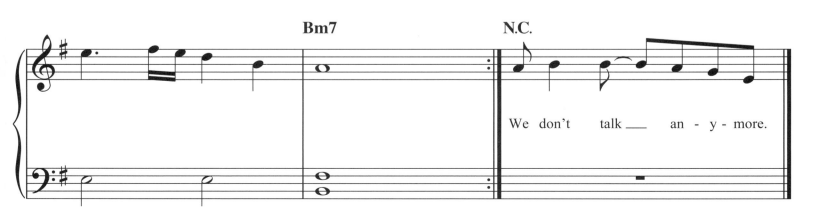

We don't talk ___ an - y - more.

TREAT YOU BETTER

Words and Music by SHAWN MENDES,
SCOTT HARRIS and TEDDY GEIGER

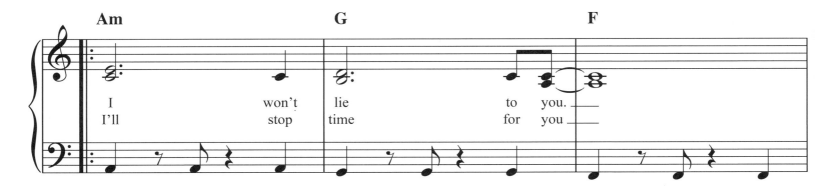

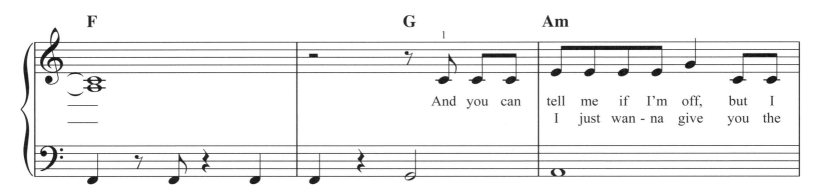

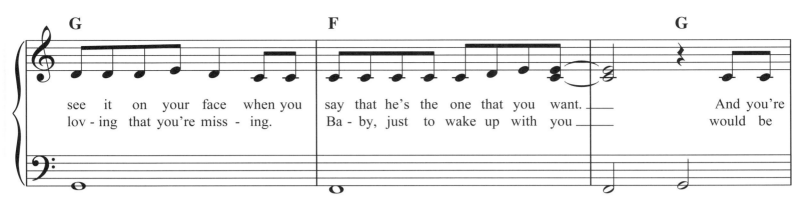

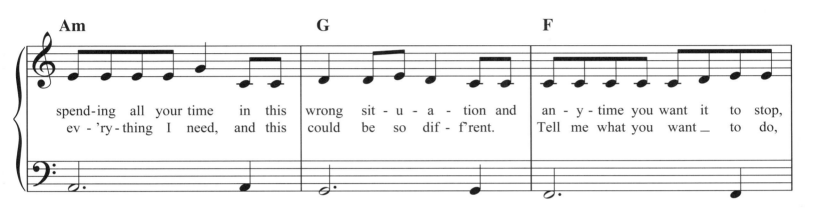

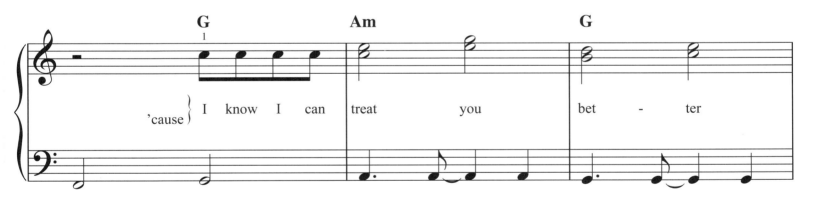

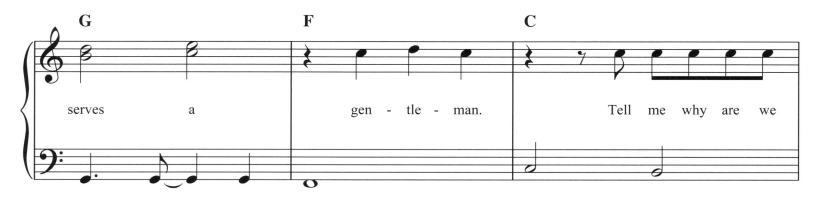

serves   a   gen - tle - man.   Tell me why are we

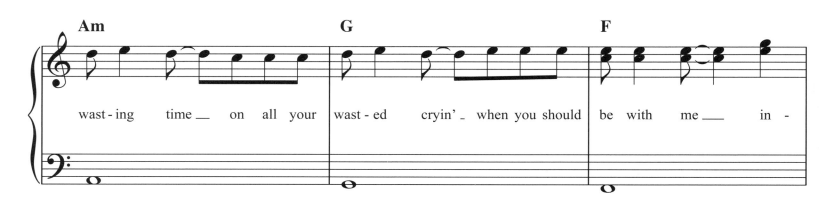

wast-ing   time __ on all your   wast-ed   cryin' __ when you should   be   with   me ___ in -

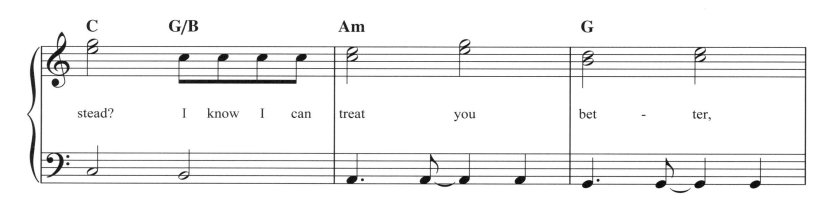

stead?   I know I can   treat   you   bet   -   ter,

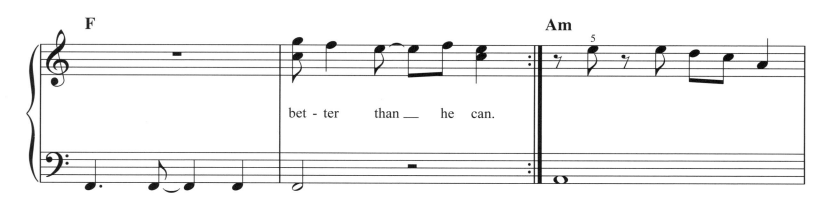

bet - ter   than __ he   can.

Bet - ter   than __ he   can.

Give   me a   sign;   take my

hand,   we'll be fine.   Prom - ise I

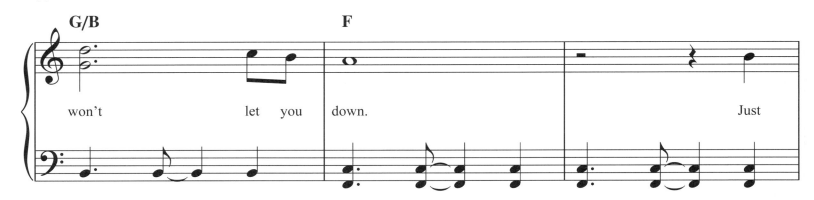

won't   let you   down.   Just

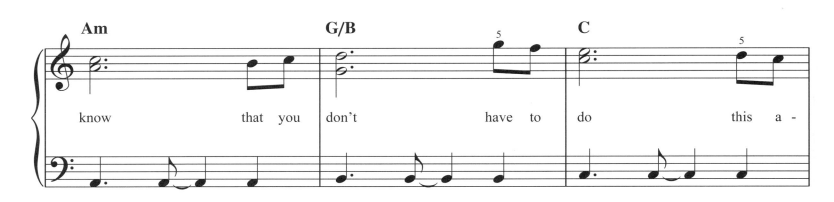

know   that you   don't   have to   do   this a -

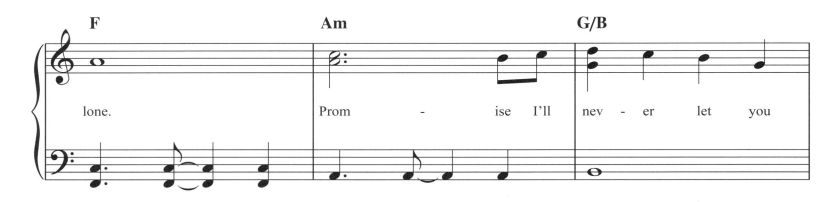

lone.   Prom - ise I'll   nev - er let   you

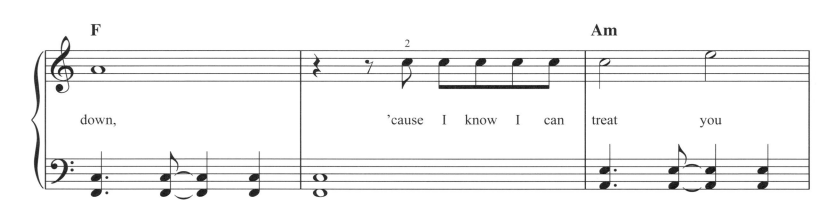

down,   'cause I know I can   treat   you

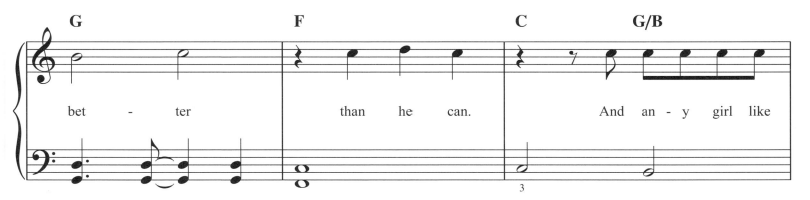

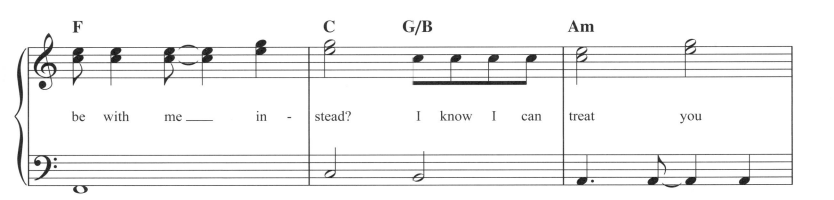

bet - ter,   bet - ter   than ___ he   can.

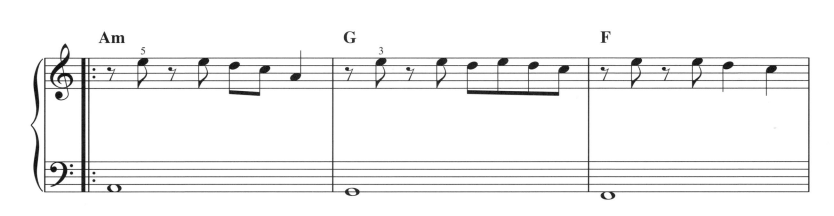

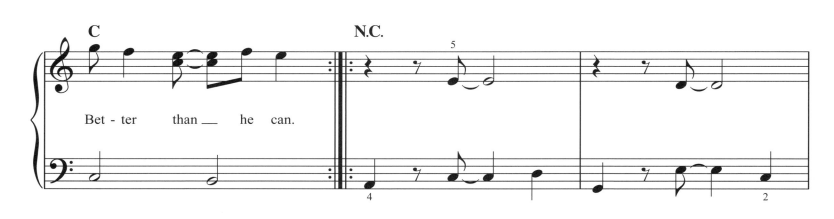

Bet - ter   than ___ he   can.